THORPENESS

Alison Brackenbury was born in 1953, from a long line of domestic servants and farm workers. She won a scholarship to Oxford, where she studied English Literature. In 1977 she moved to Gloucestershire, where she worked in a technical library, then, for twenty-three years, in her husband's tiny metal finishing company. Since her retirement in 2012, she has given readings at many festivals and other poetry events.

Alison's work has won an Eric Gregory and a Cholmondeley Award. She has broadcast frequently on Radio 3 and 4, either reading individual poems or narrating poetry programmes which she has scripted. *Gallop*, her Selected Poems, was published by Carcanet in 2019. *Thorpeness* is her eleventh collection.

Thorpeness

ALISON BRACKENBURY

CARCANET POETRY

First published in Great Britain in 2022 by
Carcanet
Alliance House, 30 Cross Street
Manchester, M2 7AQ
www.carcanet.co.uk

A CIP catalogue record for this book is
available from the British Library.

ISBN 978 1 80017 225 8

Book design by Andrew Latimer
Printed in Great Britain by SRP Ltd, Exeter, Devon

The publisher acknowledges financial
assistance from Arts Council England.

CONTENTS

NORBURY

(a hill in Gloucestershire)

I was almost hurled in the ditch.
For my first mad pony would switch
from gallop to halt in one stride.
Each ride he would swerve, fling me back
to the deep, tumbled gorge by the track.
Dark beeches hung on each side.

A hill fort? No life but its name;
'Norbury', mapped 'Iron Age'. The same
June wind conjured sweat, flies, of course.
I soothed the tossed sun-bleached mane down
by the dyke, rough grave to the town,
bones of child, wrecked fighter, horse.

What are twenty years to hill wind?
I trudge, horses out-lived. I find
the highest beech drought-struck. A rich
crest springs: orange fungus. Its throat
gapes to the war-trumpet's long note,
the lost leader's last lying which
tumbled us all in the ditch.

PURPLE HAZE

When Jimi glanced into his small attic mirror
while parting his lips, unteasing his hair,
in a candle-like glint he saw George Frideric Handel
alarmingly wigless, alarmingly there.

'What have you been taking?' said Handel to Hendrix.
'Only the usual,' Jimi replied.
'I adore your high notes,' Handel whispered. 'But listen!
You cannot cheat sleep. I went blind when I tried.

Make friends with your sound man. Then fix the fuzz pedal.
But discipline, boy! Cut your endless tracks short.'
Jimi shook his fine head. With no more breaths to meddle
George sank to roast chicken, his cellars of port.

From 1968 to 1969 Jimi Hendrix lived in an upstairs flat at 23 Brook Street,
London, next door to Handel's long-term home. He claimed that he had seen
Handel's ghost: an old man, with a grey pigtail, wearing a nightshirt.
Handel reputedly went blind because of the hours he spent copying out his
music by candlelight. His huge meals were legendary.

FERN

Does anyone wear 'buttonholes'?
We made them for the village fete.
So I was sent up to the gate

of the old man who would have gone
to 'Grammar,' if they could have bought
a crested cap, soft shoes for sport.

He passed from village desk to farm.
The one girl he had waited for
ran to an airman in the War.

His sister kept the tiny house.
A courteous, clever man, all said.
In June heat, at a long lane's end

through the blue gate, on a grass path
I stepped beneath the roses' cloud.
I saw him bend to stakes, head bowed

by billows of asparagus fern
for farmhand's collar, or the Queen,
webbed, spread like hands, its tiny veins
crisp as dead leaf, all green, so green.

CUCU

Quick April's coolest voice,
its cry came commonplace.
On farms for forty years
it flew to the same place.
Droughts, shooting leave it rare.
Now June's hard rain is falling,
so long, so late, so clear
why is the cuckoo calling?

MAY 9TH

She wears a sun hat. The child wears a sun hat,
perched before her on the bike. They dip
along their path, beside the motorway
whose trees crowd thick.

                    There is no murder,
no accident. The air stays calm.
Only that flicker in the mind forever,
of oak, lit ash, harsh reek of hawthorn, shadow.

SUNDAY ON THE COACH

It is June. Tall grasses nod. On the back seat
the last baby has hiccupped into sleep.
No one swears, nobody phones. The south wind whistles
white motorways of cow parsley and thistles.
A helicopter hangs, but does not strafe.
This afternoon the innocent are safe.

POSTCARD

But how the swifts rage!
With slash of scored sky
they write summer's page.

1975

The summer that I married
I found the pond which would
be dry one fierce year later,
fish flapping, snatched from mud.
I lay face down on grass.
The evening rose in flies,
cloud deepened on still waters.
It swam straight at my eyes,
from hidden bank or hole,
small whiskers   endless ripples.
It was the water vole.

PONY

Rough-coated, her broad nose at pockets' height,
though she was thirty-seven, she would wait
on the lush lawn they let her crop all night,
would burgle stables, barge through any gate.
Her teeth were filed, so she could mumble hay.
Her patched rugs turned the hail. But when she fell –
from all those summers, children – then, all day
they left her at her door, rugged, waiting still
the huntsman's gun, to save their last vet's bill.

WORK EXPERIENCE

Debbie. Where is Debbie? Our allocated girl,
solidly quiet, she never spoke in class,
could not find work. I sent her, in the whirl
of wind, on her new scooter, to buy cakes.
She did not fall. Then I was riding high,
I caught her in my wake. She counted cash,
she spoke at coffee. Then she got her job.
So when I had my daughter, she came by
with thick cream mittens she had made from scratch.
We bathed my baby, laugh and splash and rub,
we slid apart to lives. And I am glad
she missed the fallen years, my child turned sad.
Now the wave lifts. What is she? Fifty-three?
I hope she has no time to think of me.

SUMMIT

Rain drove at Kendal Castle
despite the hills' cupped glow.
From hawthorn heights the mistle thrush sang
'I told you   so   so   so'.

SHEPHERD BRACKENBURY

(my grandfather)

Back in the Thirties he would kill a sheep
each week, then hawk its meat round neighbouring farms.
When I was born, their hungry times had gone,
though he could still use knives in either hand.
I came once when he skinned a perished lamb
because he had another struggling one,
a triplet, trembling as it tried to stand.
He set it softly by the dead lamb's dam,
the small stained fleece knotted around its neck.
She let it feed once she had sniffed its back.
Best shoes scratched by rough straws, I learnt love meant
not glances, silky curls, but blood's raw scent.

SCYTHIAN ICE BURIAL

Sheepskin, goatskin, kidskin, sable.
Underneath a warrior's shoulder
lay the child's coat, unable

to heat, or thaw, his grave's cold power.
Were small sleeves patched for him? A son,
fevered in one summer hour?

They laid him carefully, in trust
no spade could lever earth's hard lid
no sun would pierce ground's frozen crust.

The glacier shrinks like all he did,
leaves his first coat our last ice hid.
Sheepskin, goatskin, sable, kid.

STABLE

'This is the menace test.' The vet
moves cupped hands to the pony's eye.
Now thirty, she has watched young vets

grey, like her muzzle, stoop, withdraw.
Red coat too deep for spring, she stands.
Right eye: three blinks. Left: slightly more.

From noon's high glare to stable's night
we steer her. Torch beams rake her face.
'Horses should flinch from such strong light.'

But when he points his instrument
which streams thin brightness through her eyes
some light bends back, quick rays, unspent.

I galloped her away from guns,
trotted by iced trees, only fell
because she somersaulted, once.

She slowed. Then I stopped riding, late
last year. Come spring, she crushed my foot,
last Friday, barged against a gate.

'The cataracts have reached both eyes.
The right is worse. That rectangle –
her pupil's clouded. See?' March skies

rush radiant past our dark place. 'So,
what vision's left?' His case snaps shut.
The pony sees he does not know.

GOING TO THE YARD ON MAY 19TH

I will stumble up the paddocks, where first mist blinds the air,
past the crowds of nettles, the bonfire piled with chairs.

She sleeps, four-square, alone, as she must be.
Startled in sun, her ears search dusk for me.

I buckle the headcollar. Her steps slow,
she cannot glimpse hard gates I do not own.

Summer's red coat gleams down her shoulder blade,
she rests her head on me while I brush hard,

greets her filled bucket with quick toss of head.
The yard's one robin flits to her spilt food.

Horses stand quiet when fed. She stares at skies.
No spring sun melts the cataracts from her eyes.

I click my tongue. Each calm hoof lifts. Too soon
I clean each tender frog, the sole's half-moon.

Twenty-three years. Her breath on my neck. Then
the vet must come, at half-past ten.

PONY. BLIND. AGE: THIRTY-ONE.

What I saw, still huddled by the stables
after the last injection and her crash,
was the first white sun, smoked through the pine tree,
mist's columns, clematis. Her night had passed.
First warmth flooded my face. It came to me
we rise with perfect light we cannot see.

HOPE

What will they be, our feeblest ones
who cannot stand?
Swifts who sleep upon the wind,
who never land.

NEAR LAKESIDE SCHOOL

The grey gull, rising from the fence
to the unpleasant rain,
lifts frail legs which trail to weed,
a cramped neck bent like pain.

It is the heron! If I knew
I would have fixed its old, gold eye.
Past the new school, the winter oak
its sullen wings beat high.
Its call comes harsh. The thrush drops low.
Then all the small birds cry.

BISHOP NORTON, 1932

He made my mother, short at four,
her own three-legged stool.
His childless wife stoked their small fire,
all sat as though at school.
He read the paper to them both
corn prices, fires in town,
said often, sucking his lost teeth,
'Long word!' then carried on.

Who taught my dark-eyed mother words
before teachers' tirade?
Her quick but waspish mother, hired
at fourteen, bored housemaid?
She read. The pair loved afternoons,
dazed by such cleverness.
She loved their chocolate, curved like moons,
held to their fire's hiss.

I cannot guess what fears then preyed.
War, London, work, desire?
I know that, old, she lived afraid.
She rarely left her fire.
A teacher once, she would not learn,
gave days to jams and curds.
I read the news, but silently.
I still mistrust long words.

W.J.SEAMARKS

Signature of Great-Uncle Will, Merchant Seaman, in his books

They locked you in the carriages till port.
But you had found bound poems with first pay,
you opened up your leather book at sea.

You murmured Shelley, when the wild world fought.
In fear, though you would never run away,
they locked you in the carriages till port.

Sick on the Baltic, you reached Italy,
entranced by Keats. Did hands stroke yours, at bay?
You opened up your leather book at sea

then married my great-aunt, bright-eyed, untaught,
then would not leave your cat to go away.
They locked you in the carriages till port.

Thatcher of barns, you straddled the roof-tree.
Green barley raced like spring tide on that day
you opened up your leather book at sea.

When the black cataracts swept words away
you spoke the best, then gave the rest to me.
Our bodies lock us in. Our minds steer free.
You open up your leather book at sea.

THE OLDEST TREE IN MERCOMBE WOOD

Beech tree, you are an elephant,
your crumpled bark as grey as power,
glistening and irresistible
in the small violence of a shower.
Foul water lines your long toes. Our
brief bustle will not see you through.
You are the year. We are the hour.
Green in my death, I fear for you.

THE STAFFORDSHIRE HOARD

I heave in crosses first,
the old blood gods last best.
Garnets still warm my hand,
round as her breast.

Fine filigree fell ripped from hilts,
heaped ransom for their King.
This was my share, for laboured hours,
for sorrowing.

I smell them, rain on wind.
Stiffly I climb the track.
I leave my son's toys, Roman glass,
I keep the useful sack.
Bury your treasures deep.
Never come back.

The Saxon Staffordshire Hoard contains over three thousand objects, including fragments of weapons and harness. It is thought to have been hidden in the seventh century. No one knows who buried these treasures, or why.

HOUSEHOLD GODS

They are not lotused Buddhas
clay women ripe for store.
They are two wind-bashed sparrows
who shout above our door.

WOODS, AND US

I grew up in a wood.
Well, no. I slept in bed
but spent my days by blackbirds. Rooks
cawed in my head.

I found the thrush's nest,
her cup of warm-pressed mud.
The beech trees straining to their light
sighed in my blood.

We never owned that place,
I moved at eight. And so
in town gardens, in narrowed space,
I watched trees grow

where sparrows shrilled, but neighbours
fretted for light or drains.
Now, many blackbirds later,
I find wide woods again

which few of us can grow
which no one truly owns,
new pine tips which flash red, long paths
dry as our bones.

The children storm high walks,
the broadest ground they know
beyond tall timbers, bird or fox,
our woods, where people grow.

ARRIVAL

After the gales, the bramblings breathe whistles.
Their sunset breasts shrug. They are off.
Then, from lit hawthorn, the voice of November,
the fieldfare's cross Northern cough.

ALONG THE ROAD

In Sussex, late
from the last bus
driving deep woods at night
I saw the stag
trot headlamps' beam

rut in his blood
antlered by light.

THE ALDEBURGH HERRING

I met an old man on Town Steps
who spoke to me of herring.
'Then in November we had fog
then first the sprats, then herring.

Then we spent all night on the beach
with lines and fires and fishing.
South, down the coast, they might take skate
but nothing's left here, nothing.'

The sea which floated over roofs
lay lit in bands and rolling
with every great beast we have lost
with each good season, going.

The old man shrugged his black skin coat.
On quiet waves last evening
all black and sleek on steady swell
a seal rode slowly, leaving.

Are we too late? Our waters bare,
my own tides far behind me?
But as he climbed, as cold seas fell
he smiled upon me kindly.

Long work. Short sleeps. Let white fogs grip.
May you, my unborn darling
rush skidding down each re-built step
run to the Aldeburgh herring.

THE GREEN PLOVER (LAPWING)

I see you stand in the cold mud where all
your crest and glossy colours
smudge and dull

beside the loud insistence of the gulls
by which you wait subdued
and rather small.

Emperor of fields, this is your winter life
where mud will feed you, melt the snow and hail.
Birds do not live for pride. Pulse must not fail.
The hills are stone. They whet wind to a knife.

And if this meets the mutters I have heard
from friends who moved near children by the sea
of shops, of lifts, of quiet necessity
you do not say. You wade through mud, a bird.

APOLLO, 1968

for Chris Hawkins

based on the famous photograph taken in space

They floated past the moon without a spark
of radio, the quiet before birth.
Pulsed by its cobalt seas, they watched the Earth
its perfect O, rise trustful from the dark

as we wish children might, without a mark.
See South America, whose tides of white .
shield sloths, jewelled hummingbirds which drink our light.
I was too young, sucked into my own dark.

At work, in a Tech Library, an Ark
of students, I set blue Earth on the wall
so it sailed to them, bold and beautiful.
In drawers, the plans for wind power slept in dark.

The blue sea rose, then drowned. We lost the lark.
I never dreamed that we would reach such dark.

LOST

By Coate Water, my mind believes
rain finds no end. Like three grey leaves
wet herons nestle the far shore
fearful, fond or listening for
rain's hiss to cease. While my heart grieves
wet herons wait, like three grey leaves.

ST MARY'S CHURCH, PATSHULL (REDUNDANT)

Grey, I guessed, squarely Norman,
all a village church should be?
But the landowner rebuilt it
in seventeen-forty-three.

Did George Heayes, master wheelwright,
shape spokes for his grandson?
My grandfather's grandfather, George
fed ten kids crammed in one

tied cottage. This, improbably,
still stands, though Patshull Hall
crumbled, snared by bankruptcy.
Yet Mr Brown's Greek temple

looms before a hotel's sprawl.
I ask, by screens and bedding,
for keys to the pale chapel where
a girl walked to her wedding.

Great-grandmother, Elizabeth,
eighteen and pregnant, short of breath,
passed churchyard blackbirds' mocking calls.
The future kicked at her white walls.

---

*'Tied' accommodation is provided by an employer. If the worker leaves – or
loses – their job, they normally lose their home.*
*'Mr Brown' is 'Capability Brown', whose landscapes in Patshull Park have
survived, mainly in a golf course.*
*Elizabeth, my mother's grandmother, was married at St Mary's. Her father,
George Heayes, is buried there. I found no headstone for him.*

ELDER

Your cup of flowers, a dish of cream.
Your scent, high summer's bitter dream.
How pickers cram you in their sack!

How, from that elderflower champagne
my great-aunt made, one night of rain
you fired corks through her wardrobe's back!

Your own wine, mulled by months of heat,
glints in lax fruits, on fresh-hung sheets
signed purple by each bird that flies.

Yet your rank strength may turn to use.
Your stinking leaves, if dangled loose,
swish stingers from a pony's eyes.

How you haunt low yards! Overhead
sun sinks, ignored. Once all lies dead
iced moon, your sister, lifts instead
your New Year's flower, behind our shed.

THE DISUSED STABLES

Her practical calm partner says
while he checks each bare stall by night,
how, through roof's gaps, a cool draught blows,
how, at storm's height, he feels his neck
nudged sharply by the pony's nose.

MEETING 1919

between my Great Uncle Sidney and the wife of a Buckinghamshire
squire

'Well, Wright,' she called in the raw wind, 'we heard
that you were safely home. Now, I suppose
you'll work for us again?' When pantry boy,
Sid stood at one a.m., still scraping grease
off dinner party plates. 'I've had four years
with sergeants shouting at me what to do.
I've not come home to be bossed round by you.'
She turned for Chicheley Hall without a word.

ETHEL: SHOTS FROM A LIFE

Tweeds, dogs, sharp glance, a proudly whispered name,
widow, turned archaeologist,
our village brush with fame.

Her trapped mid-years, with pension but no spouse
were spent indoors with 'Ma and Pa'
whose rows split their dark house.

Young, snapped as governess – her only bolt –
she stood slim in her sweeping skirt,
reached high to kiss their colt.

Her reckless journal mocked her friend who lazed
while Ethel worked; friend's brother, George,
how lionised and praised.

At their June fete, no children under feet,
how briskly she dodged lanky George
she had vowed not to meet.

How trap and pony whirled, past stars, past forge.
By elder's moon, beneath rough rugs,
how she held hands with George.

This poem is based partly on the published diaries of Ethel Rudkin (1893-1985). She was a pioneering folklorist and archaeologist, who did not always receive full credit for her earliest discoveries. I met her when I was a child, in the small Lincolnshire village where we both grew up.
George, her husband, joined the army in the First World War, then died of flu.

FOUND

Why is my bookmark near the bed, just as
a seed lies where it lands?
Because I fell asleep. You took the book
gently, from my hands.

MATCHED

Red kite   soars winter acres   bankrupt king
ice over ground   frost in the trees   snow under wing

ON THE EDGE

By their late lemon leaves, fat sloes
hang strangely sparse. One fierce cough, close.
High in the thorns, with black-streaked breast,
a tall bird, Northern flank smudged red,
buff eye-stripe flashed across its head,
lights dim November, sun at rest.
It shuns town, yet is driven there
by cold it fled, Siberian air.
Redwing in street? Admire. Beware.

CAR PARK, CHRISTMAS EVE

Red, quivered sky, first rain sign, blurred to purple,
drops rinsed around a glass before the rest.
Wrapped bottles clink. How unpoured wine tastes best.

Amy Mary, labourer's child,
feared for food when harvests failed.
What did her mended stocking hold,
when thatched snow lit the house?
'An apple and an orange
and a sugar mouse'.

Factory's overtime revoked,
her children chose. Marge? Or jam?
Christmas hopes, at tea, provoked
Amy Mary's list. Her house
hummed along. My mother sang
'AND a sugar mouse!'

I met Christmas on the hop,
with Fairtrade chocolate; one lean year
a toy dog from the local shop.
In City suit, in our small house,
suddenly my daughter chants
'and a sugar mouse'...

Grey, with loot, I bounce the bus.
At dawn, in dream, before the trussed
presents, rain, descend on us,
I nibble, in that kind dark house,
on the crystal crust
of my sugar mouse.

TOADSTOOLS, NEW YEAR

By Cranham's road, where ceaseless traffic flows,
they perched, on awkward toes,
beside bleached hogweed, mud.

The lowest fought. Their orange lords leapt free.
White ribs, fanned to a tree,
matched palest clouds. Paths led

our stony scramble to a wind-shocked height.
There Gloucester rose to light,
each tower wore mist's slow hood.

By ferns, persistent streams, I thought of them,
gold, amber, apricot on one small stem.
They burned the brightest thing in all the wood.

JANUARY 1ST

Flashed by my torch, white petals,
fine rain which leaves no mark.
So this is our new winter,
roses in the dark.

J.

One ledge. One slip. All gone, at twenty-two.
The sudden pain flies past me, with your cry,
from mother, brother, everyone you knew
beyond the mountain and its steady sky.

I met you once. I handed you a prize.
Did I help kit you for that wrecking climb?
How slight you stood. You hid behind quick eyes.
You would not be a lawyer, lay waste time.

Did you waste all? The young start frail and bold,
the bruised white violet of my winter hedge.
You wrote of places 'beautiful and cold'.
You stood that cold, until one icy edge.

You hand the cup to me. Stiff-shouldered, old,
I sip your sky. I shuffle from your ledge.

THE QUEEN'S APARTMENTS IN THE PALACE OF HOLYROODHOUSE

Should Scotland's towers rise lordly,
the young Queen's skirts sweep wide?
Steps dip and twist so meanly
a child must duck inside.
How close they press, our life's rooms,
as sweat, which lines fine clothing,
as intimate as locks.
Upright, with careful bearing,
no thread of red hem trailing,
the Queen waits for John Knox.

She will flee her baby, let
her twisted husband die,
her soft musician butchered,
a second thug to try.
How straight she stands in freedom,
dances lilt her veins like rage.
Bloomed candles light her eyes,
while Knox's wife, a daughter's age,
slowly turns her Bible page.
He climbs with heavy thighs.

He speaks for the tired poor.
Her petticoats sigh silk.
Careless, he will thump the floor
while her breasts ache with milk.
While righteous dark rules his night,
must her light-voiced pleas still lose?
How boldly she declares:
crooked stone slips from your shoes,
quick time gutters, you must choose,
John Knox stamps up the stairs.

These are the apartments of Mary Queen of Scots (1542–87). Her musician David Rizzio was murdered in front of her while she was pregnant. Her husband, Henry Darnley, was also murdered. Mary then married the Earl of Bothwell.
John Knox (1513–72) was the founder of the Presbyterian Church of Scotland. He and Mary had several stormy meetings in the Palace of Holyroodhouse.

TERRITORIES

Where lemon melts to mustard
its song a throaty clamour,
to every month a new moon,
each hedge, a yellowhammer.

MR HILL AND ME

Do not catch measles. For you cannot read,
or could not, back in nineteen fifty-nine.
Then, as my sight slid from me at high speed
they told me to walk home, alone, since schools
knew no one they might ring. My village shimmered.
There were no cars, no strangers, so, no rules.

Since we lived in a far house in a wood,
I walked, unsteadily, up Middle Street
where Mr Hill, the old roadsweeper, stood
in his own sigh of dust. But when I spoke
my parched throat gave no sound. His brush hissed on.
I shivered, May noon's ghost, small wave that broke,

then crept up Hollowgate Hill, high-hedged Long Lane,
to bed, below cool yews. They kept me dark.
How mind blots boredom, dims old scabs and pain!
Yet, fevered, I swim back, to noon, to days
where Mr Hill, while dogs and sparrows sleep,
sweeps histories' hot dust to one bright haze.

They were, in fact, the woods of Gloucestershire.
Stone shacks, once keeper's, shepherd's, now too damp,
too far for the few farm-hands, were let cheap
to painters who would risk an oil lamp,

to sculptors who might steal their landlord's wood.
It was the Sixties. They were there. Who would
remember them? One woman wrote a book,
named a bedraggled poet who mistook

beech trees for gods. His family still owned
the Manor. In hill-wind, through his mind's flicker
he flew past gods' streamed arms on his old bike
down to his village to appoint the Vicar.

One tribe, descended from Augustus John,
lived with cracked slates at Needlehole. Along
the hedges, in strong Hill House, in the wilds
of Hilcot Wood, camped Connie, pots and child.

They watched the combines storm the hedgeless fields.
They learned how stakes blocked badger setts, like laws.
The stubble ploughed, first frost thick on their glass,
they packed for London, locked their rotten doors.

But in green May, Ernie, the keeper, brought
young lettuce for the new beds she had worked.
(The cat dug those.) He took her nephews out,
showed them sharp prints of deer he would not shoot.

Her book won prizes. Then she moved away.
Where Ernie, who had teased her, strolled on Sunday
to pose for shots, blue jay's plumes in his hat,
he trudged the deepest drifts. He saved her cat.

6.59

Soon our sun must blink, eclipsed. Fog crouches
on the streets' worn roofs, their silver birches,
the thrown down bikes, the neighbour's broken fence
on which the blackbird flourishes. No sense
may match a song. I find, bought for this day,
two thin black lenses framed by card. Will they
save tender veins in blaze we strain to see?
Mist and the blackbird tell me, patiently,
how small I sit, how soon vast dusk must drop
on sun, how everything I love must stop.

KING'S CROSS HOTEL

The blackest pigeons in London
court by my chimney pot.
The sirens sing all night, of course.
Unsleeping windows throb. It's hot.
At dawn, I swear, I hear a horse
which breaks into a trot.

'AUNT MARGARET'S PUDDING'

*Based on a black-covered handwritten notebook of recipes from
Dorothy Eliza Barnes, 'Dot', my grandmother. When I knew
Dot, she was a Lincolnshire shepherd's wife. But, as a young
woman, she had been an Edwardian professional cook.*

Start

Page one: 'Aunt Margaret's Pudding'.
Take half a pound of flour,
three ounces lard (or butter), egg,
milk, sugar, baking powder.
Spread jam in basin, summer gleam.
Poke fire! For ninety minutes, steam.

Dot took for granted custard seas,
in which all puddings swam –
yellow as straw, farmworkers' food.
In frost, the men tramped home.
Moon glittered. No one knew how lard
would line and leave their arteries hard.

When I came home and you worked late,
our workshop gloomed with cold,
I bought flour from the corner shop
sacked cupboards for old bowls.
Softly the mixture dropped. I too
spooned Margaret's hot jam sponge for you.

All change

In schoolgirl hand and blackest black
you scratched down with your steel nib
'Puzzle Pudding, Feather Cake',
in neat fast script, no time to think.
Now sky-blue strays into the mix,
light as fire through kindling sticks.
Pencil races. 'Elderberry'.
Then biro shakes. No more splashed ink.

'B.P.' was baking powder. Why?
Did slick self-raising come too late?
Nor did you have penicillin,
Pethidine, or the Welfare State.
'Cake with dried egg'. You barely paused,
queued, improvised, cooked through two wars.
'Slow oven.' By my birth, you could
swap coal for cooker, need not wait.

Still you kept adding recipes,
lighter, not heavy, blue, not black.
From *Woman's Own* came 'Chocolate Cake'.
The '60s cooled upon your rack.
With sister, daughter dead, you made
fine curds, great pies, long table laid.
Why did you never show me this?
'Beat four eggs well.' Do not look back.

High-class food

Both my grandmothers were of age
to stuff fat sausages with sage,

Lincolnshire's herb which calms the blood.
They could make dumplings sweet with suet,

slash egg-white with a knife till thick,
plate shoulder-poised, Victorian trick,

but never dreamed of kneading bread.
They ran to bakers' vans instead.

Yet when strange men tramped round the farms
to beg for work, in '30s storms,

Dot, between her jobs, would pour
them tea beside her fire before

sending them out in rain well-fed
on home-cured bacon and white bread.

Ingredients

Carrots kept Christmas pudding plain.
No gold leaf flattered Nottingham.
'Choclate' – you wrote, brisk, young.
What sweetness touched your tongue?

Your first friends were cornflour, ground rice.
Your middle age still sang with spice,
spooned, generous to a fault.
Cinnamon. Ginger. 'Salt'?

Steam smudged your letters. 'Leather Cups'?
I squint. The words are: 'Quaker Oats'.
Your trust in brand names shone.
King, Country, only one.

You knew 'dessert'. You wrote
the old name: 'cocoanut'.
Past bright 'Treacle', I see
the dark Imperial tree.

A married student, money short,
I spooned rough ground rice at the start –
strong, workaday, low cost –
like all the tastes we lost.

Dot

But you were tiny. Not one toe
could stretch from sofa to the floor.
Unwise to marry a tall man? For
the fourth child left you bed-bound, so
kind neighbours cooked. Your eyes were weak
yet blue as harebells. You would go
sleepless, to cram old trunks with cake
the men took to the Royal Show.

I have one picture, leather-bound:
you as a young, still-anxious cook,
flowered velvet in your collar's tuck.
Like food, you could make cash go round.
Only your hair grew wild. Its fine
strong waves defied your careful buns.
French marigolds by your washing line
met cabbage, hoed by husband, sons.

You never cut your springing hair.
Time washed past you like rain, your skin
so soft a child's lips would sink in.
My face, rough from hill wind, stays bare
of blusher, gloss. No powder tins
littered your rooms. I stay up, too,
cook, type, as horizons dim.
My father said I looked like you.

Summer fruit

You whisked meringues, light pancakes lest
Madam woke bored. You did not write
two recipes I loved the best

that dark blancmange, named 'Chocolate Mould',
which, young paid cook, you once coaxed whole
from fluted copper's fragrant gold,

then spooned, for us, from your gilt dish.
African nights caressed slow tongues.
We tasted empires, bitter, rich.

How could you find fruit in that flat
unflowered land? Air bloomed. You caught
the Barton bus, in your best hat.

Plum jam set August. Amber simmered
to slow taste, whole, spooned on warm sponge
as boots came off, Orion glimmered.

Summer, you said, for that Great War,
was like none after or before,
the loveliest you ever saw.

Samphire

'Halfway down
Hangs one that gathers samphire—dreadful trade!
Methinks he seems no bigger than his head.'
King Lear, Act 4, Scene 6

My grandmother could cook it, for
she grew up by that dangerous shore
where the sea skulked without a wall

where I have seen it, tough as grass,
where silent men with rods trooped past
its salty ranks, without a glance.

Lear's gatherer hangs perilously.
Why? So much is closed to me.
Did Shakespeare ever hear the sea?

Once, said my father, far inland,
from friend or stall, one clutch was found,
steamed, in my grandmother's great pan.

Later, a leaflet from a shop
claimed they could 'source it'. In its place
stood peppered cress – another gap.

Yet how it waved in late sea-light –
stalks I will never taste, but make
tenderly dark, my coast's sly snake,
salt on my tongue, before I wake.

LINCOLNSHIRE WATER

Here is strong land, whose grass
does not spill foaming milk,
where I still hear, in February,
taps hiss cold silk.

You found a hobby: funerals.
The village taxi (Mr Hall's),
sailed to your door to take you there
while your son rode to the Game Fair
one holiday. You unpeeled notes
from your upright, moth-guarded coats.

Sometimes you crossed two towns by bus.
My doting father frowned at fuss.
'They're all Dad's family. And why
doesn't she go when they're alive?'
I think he missed the point. For sure
you met them at the wake before,

talked in front rooms, with creaking floors,
chewed pastries heavier than yours.
The women chose their corners. Men
just held by suits, tears dried by sun,
were spared from tractor seat or forge,
named, like my father, Harold, George,

the Cousins. So when you returned,
your bus ticket and black coat earned
one radiant hour at Sunday tea,
telling my father all you'd seen.
'You know him, Harold!'
                          'The butcher?'
                                        'No,
they say he flitted. Nelly's Joe –'

You ticked them off on fingers, rapt,
as my bored father's best shoes tapped,
then gazed into the *Chronicle*
which sang you each fresh funeral.
Children were sheltered. I – kept out –
did not see you flit from your house.

Fred lived for only two more years.
With funeral hands too full for tears
I swayed, in heels, down backyard steps,
then offered ham, my mother's cakes,
to tall men, from crew-yard or forge,
called Harold, mostly (sometimes George).

ON HORKSTOW HILL

House-moving was called 'flitting' and
your flitting crossed half Lincolnshire
until your shepherd husband saw
the best show flock, on Horkstow Hill.

'Well, Fred is married to the sheep.'
You had your house and men to keep
but could be sometimes lonely, while the deep
horse chestnut shadows swept the sill.

I came to visit for a day.
Red conker flowers blew past your gate
where Toots, the old dog, waited, chained
by the back door, too stiff for hills.

The morning washed us like a dream.
I must have read. You chopped, boiled, cleaned,
scoured pans, quick cook. Small windows flared,
late summer sun soared on the hill.

'We'll have a walk', you told me then.
'Go up the hill and find the men.'
You clamped your hat on like the Queen.
Your village slept, one street. Yet still

women came out, to nod to you,
to ask about my life. I knew
I was your prize show lamb. But soon
we caught the wind and climbed the hill.

Although I wanted most to keep
close by the men, the half-clipped sheep,
I saw broad Humber shine beneath,
and small heartsease, at corn's edge, spill.

I never realised you were old.
You marched back, cooked huge tea. In folds
muddied as love, the Humber rolled
as we climbed Horkstow Hill.

YOUR GREAT-GRANDDAUGHTER COOKS

If offered peppered rocket leaf;
green olive oil you used to keep
for ears; light buns with blueberries;
smooth pasta; soft Italian cheese;
German red cabbage, simmered hours;
sage leaf fried crisp –
                  if, lit by flowers,
your plate was set, what would you do?
Taste each fresh mouthful, wonderingly.
Then ask her for the recipe.

BEFORE THEY WAKE

Red sun hangs perfect, terrible as war,
the blink of grief, the glass which holds no more.
Then gold throbs, the unbearable sun's eye,
magnolia whitens, boiler smoke streams by
till muffled cloud and muddled radiance give
that dull but blessed light by which we live.

THE TRAIN: 1993, 2020

The Russian train has two young women guides,
Katya, slim Helen. Flowered shirt-cloth hides
paunches on the young Mafia. Knives slide
all day on the potato-peeler's knee
between compartments. Sasha grins, strides past,
six feet of engineer. Steam-whistles blast.
The quiet, helpful man who boarded last,
with fluent German, may be KGB.

We see the wooden towns. We glimpse a moose,
churches with incense, dead pools like a bruise
by slender broken birches. Who would choose
to live here? Fresh food for her child to eat
is Helen's aim. Why, on the final day
do sobs shake her small breasts, to the train's sway?
Sasha, shrunk suddenly, stows tools away
before he meets the murderous Moscow street.

*

Sickness. Each night I board, in home-locked dream,
a fearful train. A boy in bundled green
who has no papers, leaps out, rolls down scree,
races past startled cows. The wet glass streams,
I grip my silvered strip of pills. I know
I must find the young girl, whose vivid glow
means fever. Calm, awake, would I do so?
I doubt it. We act better in our dreams.

I wake, then shiver. The March light blows wild.
How many died? How old is Helen's child?

I must feed cats, next, count the tinned peas, piled
against our hungers, the forgotten rain.
I could use Sasha's tools. Who will bring pills?
In each room sleepers wake, while pure sun spills.
The radio leaks facts. The kettle fills.
Rocked deeper, scared, we still must ride this train.

WILLOW PATTERN

a lockdown walk

Town's edge. A lane. A bridge. A field
marched by the battered stumps of maize,
lit by hills, broad as the moon.
The cracks in April clay will yield
rich oyster shells to feed poor days;
pipes; pigs' skulls; best, we find soon,

smashed pottery. And most is blue,
slipped from quick hands, a child's, a maid's,
to floor. Were harsh words spoken?
I brush a latticed rim while you
scoop one white scrap whose two blue birds,
smudged lovers, soar unbroken.

In Victorian England, oysters were a cheap food.
The 'Willow pattern' on china depicts the story of two lovers, one rich, one poor.
After death, the lovers are re-united as birds.

THE SIGNS OF SPRING

Do not, please, mention daffodils,
though my sense staggers at their scent,

hot as a furnace. By next light
their flags are ruined, shredded, rent.

And do not once refer to lambs
which fled from us, two frantic girls.

Grandfather, shepherd, stooped. Stroke, shocked,
the grey, bare skin, tight, greasy curls.

From marbled leaves, small spiders skid.
They skate brief sun's pools on eight feet.

Their pattered dance trusts frosts will not
burn mild dusk blue, freeze Venus white.

What delicate waver weaves the yard
to daffodils, seedlings, soil fresh dug?

The tiny ticking pulse of earth,
the surest sign of spring. The slug.

MOTHERING SUNDAY

I heard the high raw crying of the geese.
I could not see them, which I did not mind.
But smaller in the small yard, I stood sad
since, for the first time, I was left behind.

THE LAST DAY OF MARCH

Spiked blackthorn can prick horses' feet,
pierce tender soles. Then poison swells.
Yet each frank flower sets freckled silk
against March skies of steel and milk.

Lean close. Their amber stamens dart,
a green space plunges to each heart,
from which the small bloomed fruits will grow
a hedgerow's purpled lips, the sloe.

Guarding the long edge of the field
on which the farmer hopes to build,
each banked bush flares its fires of white
before the oaks can break to light.

A farmer told me, springs ago,
of 'blackthorn winter'. Soon, I know
beside this blossom, cars will slow
for ice, each lamb lie veiled with snow.

MID-MARCH

Although the oak and ash spread bare
the buzzard's collar turns to snow.
Bedraggled in magnificence
pheasants, who hid from hushed guns, go.

MARCH 4TH

I heave back the bathroom window.
The catch is stiff and, like me, old.
I would like to let in the crescent moon.
She is so slender, and must be cold.

WEDNESDAY ON THE 97

Like family you complain about but love,
I am at home with buses. This is prompt.
At every stop it dawdles in the sun.

I do not phone, read, talk. I simply sit.
I watch deep sycamores dip to the south
as if the whole day is a cat that purrs
and I the tongue, vibrating in its mouth.

WELLINGTON SQUARE

Eight blackbirds in a square
so early, found so late,
a bus, come unexpectedly,
an unlocked gate,

no password, no keypad,
one sweep of mown grass where
by copper beech, by holm oak
sheltered from sky and square

eight blackbirds of all ages,
all sizes, flecked with fawn
or smouldered black, flicked pages
of leaf. Chill shock of dawn

had not deterred the worms which hung
from each beak in wet wreaths.
Birds hunted, too intent
to rise from paths like breaths.

Only when a dog ran
when heat smoked from the sun
I turned from ghost to human
from eight blackbirds to none.

THE COUNTRY WRITERS

(Edward Thomas, Richard Jefferies, and many others)

They lingered by cool dairies' yellow milk,
which we never dreamed of or saw.
Children sipped froth beside the hot stacks, through
a hollow straw.

They scared a hundred sparrows from eared corn,
woke to their thrushes' common song.
The line of rooks which flared the sky to roost
stretched five miles long.

First, all they wanted was to tramp all day
out in the air, though soaked or cold.
They rented rooms; but the old farmer died.
Those hills were sold.

My shepherd grandfather got up at dawn
so he could pause, and watch young badgers play.
They wrote in London, fought deadlines,
smoked life away.

Were woods, the wren in bedroom, true, or just
a dream behind a hurt child's eyes?
Today I saw a hundred peacocks whirl,
swallows fill skies.

I did not dream of butterflies, but sought
in hot town nights, before first engines' hum,
my visa for your country to which I
have not yet come.

'MY LADY NEWCASTLE... IN A LARGE BLACK COACH.'

(Samuel Pepys)

Her name was Margaret. William made it 'Pegs'.
Glimpsed young, at Court in exile, never poor,
Lady-in-Waiting, she had not looked for
this nervous Duke. Yet, wrecked by Marston Moor,
he loved a girl who lived on boiled eggs.

He pawed her half-grown maids. She failed to note them.
Back in shocked England, by each ruined house,
he reined Spain's stallions round his 'Riding House'.
Men mocked the books her Duke thought marvellous.
'Here's the crime!' he raged. 'A Lady wrote them.'

Could wild Margaret make one decent line?
Did freedom spoil her, while fresh maids advanced?
She scrawled each day. Young, costly stallions danced.
Yet she scared thieving stewards into line,

raked in each rent for William's sake, maintained
his painted nymphs. His Duchess dodged the Court.
She picked pied silks, while scientists throbbed her thought.
Death called, quick editor. The Duke's tears rained.
The black coach rocked. Its lead pair slowed, well-trained.

Margaret Cavendish, Duchess of Newcastle, (1623–73), published at least twenty-nine books.
William Cavendish, who supported the King in the English Civil War, went into exile after the disastrous battle of Marston Moor.

THOMAS HARDY SENDS AN EMAIL

I need slide no confessions under doors
where they are brushed by farm boots under mats.
Bored girls buy no new-fangled cards. How that
Valentine throbbed, foamed with silk hearts, false flowers!
Forget notes, in a stiff, slow, childish hand.
I flick the quick screens I must understand,
electronic errors

when one click sends the secret you must keep
to the whole office, and the office cat,
when a lone drunk, locked in a basement flat,
can stop a heart with threats of knives and rape,
when the young man, whose smile dissolves your screen,
asks for your password and your username.
I could not make this up.

Listen. My dark keys tap. Let me confess
my long books lied to you. For I was Fate.
My messages? All false. Desire, too late
re-programmed me. In anger, I hung Tess.
Old wordings, slights, my grand house slip from me.
I log out, choose. A fiddler I must be,
whose tunes bemuse and bless.

DIRECTIONS

(Jenny Joseph, 2008)

'These maps will not help,'
I fan three, starred with ink.
So you bristle truth
As a cattle fence, wreathed with stiff wire.

'Do not turn off here!'
But you list every sign
'Beds, Sofas, Sale.' What shall we talk of,
Sofa or bed? You can flow on for hours.

'Look left. Watch for cars
Sweeping up Brimscombe Hill,'
Your bath is scrubbed white.
Pumpkins swell watered leaf,

'There are dozens of ways
Over Rodborough Hill.'
Why did you leave London?
Who do you love?

'The cows walk straight at you,'
Your cellar is damp.
Letters lap you, like leaves:
I do not know your dark.

'Turn right, by Tom Long's Post,
Immediately left,'
You are wise as the mist.
I am not worth your shoe.

'You are in Windmill Road,'
You wait, twenty years on,
With your bent hips, sharp eyes,
Firm with children, your gate.
I shall follow your maps
For each twist of the road.
I am your good pupil,
I shall be late.

JENNY JOSEPH

(1932–2018)

When we met, you were still angry about 'Warning'.
'Can't they put something else in their anthologies?' you said.
'Yes,' I agreed. 'Your love poems. Your ballads.'
Like Bramleys on your deep stone sill, you mellowed.
How patiently you prised each wormhole out.
But you, who saw so much, first lost your sight,
then your strong back, so you bore years in bed.

In the old bus station in Birmingham,
the one where oily water sulked in pools,
each sandwich seemed a threat, I met a widow
who told me of her husband's death, still raw.
By bitter tea (just why, I don't recall)
she laughed and quoted 'Warning'. When I told you,
you asked 'And did you tell her that you knew me?'
your face like your granddaughter's, tilted, glad.
Then I said 'No'. At midnight, in my new
now fruitless kitchen, how I wish I had.

'HONEYMOON'

from the memoirs of Helen, widow of the poet, Edward Thomas

They fled, by train, to a poacher
Edward named 'Dad'. His own father
made the Civil Service, rather

than risky Dad's wood-cottage. Green
lit thatch like oaks, the emerald sheen
of pheasants' necks Dad wrung, unseen.

Helen woke to a stitched quilt, lace,
wet primrose by her breakfast place,
Dad's wife with bonny, gap-toothed face.

The old voice told her, 'Life turns hard.
You must stew turnips, eke out lard.'
Then Edward called her from the yard.

They swam unclothed, no thought of wrong,
sang in broad lamplight, song on song.
They would live so their whole lives long.

But when both longed, in flight, to stay,
Granny, with Dad, had moved away
near Swindon's red-bricked railway.

Edward and Helen Thomas were still unmarried when they stayed with 'Dad' and 'Granny' Uzzell.

AFTER

(Helen and Edward Thomas)

But let us think of them at last
as they might always want to be.
The boy with the soft voice. The girl
who swung bare toes from a cherry tree.

Helen's tree-climbing, in her father's garden, is described in her memoir, Under Storm's Wing *(Carcanet, 1997).*

PACKING THE PAPERS

It seems to me for the first time, sadly,
they have all gone, the ones who could tell.
Our obituaries, if any, I note gladly,
must come from those who never knew us well.

CHARLES DICKENS AT HOME

Bombs, cranes made his grand houses
mere rubble under feet
but not their narrow first door,
48 Doughty Street.

Kind Catherine clasped the baby
Dickens set up his desk.
He rattled sherry bottles.
She counted out the eggs.

The basement stairs could break knees.
Her belly twitched, stretched sore.
Charles frowned across the garden
Oliver asked for more.

Slowly, Kate shuffled menus,
sweet salvage of her life.
'What Shall We Have for Dinner?'
He wrote 'Is She his Wife?'

Spring Soup, then Vermicelli.
The hospital fund. Grey curls.
Oxtail, Mock Turtle. Hare Soup.
The house for fallen girls.

His favourite child was Katey,
who painted, laughed, dared turn
to snatch the frail reading desk
her father chose to burn.

Behind his tallest, last house,
with Catherine packed away
he lit his bundled letters.
'I have no more to say.'

The profile of his actress
shows tension, sharp-lipped grace,
not Catherine's muddled ringlets
not unlike Katey's face.

'We live in all our houses.'
ash whispers to the sleet.
Lime buds tap bedroom windows,
upstairs, in Doughty Street.

In 1851, under the name of Lady Maria Clutterbuck, Catherine published a book of meal plans:
What Shall We Have for Dinner?
Is She his Wife? *is the title of an early play by Dickens.*

Dickens had a desk built for his reading tours. When illness forced him to stop, he planned to burn this.

Catherine and Charles Dickens had ten children. Dickens separated from his wife in 1858. In the last years of his life, he had a secret relationship with a young actress, Ellen Ternan.

'I have no more to say' is the final sentence of a letter from Dickens to his publishers, Evans and Bradbury.
He quarrelled with them over their support for Catherine.

FLASH

In Kenya, to bleached branch it came,
noon's bird, Malachite kingfisher.
Even the broad beak borrowed flame.

At Rousham – was the Cherwell there? –
with friends who, later, trekked through hell,
sun's amber, fallen skies lit air.

Near Oxford, by the stained canal
your latest love turned unkind. You
watched rainstorms fade. Wings burned banks blue.

When the drab days unwind you
do not put streams behind you.
Wait for the light to blind you.

SHINGLE

Will I get to Thorpeness?
Well, not today
since my feet clash the beach
the other way.
A young brown gull veers, pipes
its thin cry of distress.

All the bright screens cry 'Rain'.
A mermaid's purse,
a black pouch lies, fish eggs
that deep sea nursed.
Vainly, I skim it back.
Rain beats my nose and chin.

In tall streets, low clouds press.
Three swallows snatch
a gust, a breath, last fly.
Small voices catch
land's end, storm's edge, whirl high
far, far beyond Thorpeness.

ACKNOWLEDGEMENTS

Magazines, podcasts and websites

Acumen, Ambit, ARTEMISpoetry, Caught by the River, Diversifly podcast, Fair Acre Press, *Finished Creatures, Magma, New England Review, Oxford Poetry, New Boots and Pantisocracies, Poetry Birmingham Literary Journal, Poetry Review, Poetry Salzburg, Poetry Wales, Stand, The London Magazine, The North, The New Statesman, The Reader, The Spectator, The Times Literary Supplement, Under the Radar, Wild Court, Words for the Wild, WRITE where we are NOW.*

Anthologies

Aunt Margaret's Pudding, Happen*Stance* Press, 2018, *Beyond Spring* by Matthew Oates, Fair Acre Press, 2017, *Christmas Crackers*, Candlestick Press, 2017, *For the Silent*, ed. Ronnie Goodyer, Indigo Dreams, 2019, *Giving Voice*, ed. Ilse Pedler, BAHVS & CAM4animals, 2019, *Locked Down* ed. Susan Jane Sims, Poetry Space, 2021, *Places of Poetry* ed. Andrew McRae, Oneworld, 2020, *Poems for the Year 2020*, ed. Merryn Willliams, Shoestring, 2021, *Quartet: the Four Seasons*, ed. Deborah Gaye, Avalanche, 2018, *Reflected Light* ed. Joy Howard, Grey Hen Press, 2020, *Spring of the Muses,* ed. Deborah Gaye, Avalanche, 2019, *The Tree Line*, ed. Michael McKimm, Worple Press, 2017.

'Apollo 1968' and 'Before they wake' were broadcast on BBC Radio 6 Music, on Chris Hawkins' show.

'All change', 'High-class food', 'On Horkstow Hill', 'Start', 'Summer Fruit', 'The Lincolnshire Chronicle', and 'Your great-granddaughter cooks' were broadcast on BBC Radio 4 on 17 June 2018, in a feature called *What Sweetness Touched Your Tongue?*, produced by Julian May.

'The signs of spring' was broadcast on BBC Radio 4, in March 2021, on *Front Row*, produced by Simon Richardson.

'W.J.Seamarks' was broadcast on BBC Radio 4, in September 2018, on *Front Row*, produced by Julian May.

'Charles Dickens at home', 'Purple Haze', 'The Queen's apartments in the Palace of Holyroodhouse' and 'The Staffordshire Hoard' were broadcast on BBC Radio 4, in June 2020, on *Front Row*, produced by Julian May.